45 Macaroni Recipes for Home

By: Kelly Johnson

Table of Contents

- Classic Macaroni and Cheese
- Baked Macaroni with Cheddar and Breadcrumbs
- Creamy Alfredo Mac and Cheese
- Spicy Buffalo Macaroni and Cheese
- Lobster Mac and Cheese
- Pesto Cavatappi
- Tex-Mex Macaroni Casserole
- Three-Cheese Macaroni Gratin
- Bacon and Jalapeño Mac and Cheese
- Broccoli and Cheddar Macaroni Bake
- Macaroni Carbonara
- Chili Mac
- Greek Macaroni Salad
- Sundried Tomato and Feta Macaroni
- Truffle Mac and Cheese
- Macaroni with Roasted Red Pepper Sauce
- Spinach and Artichoke Macaroni Casserole
- Taco Macaroni Skillet
- Macaroni Goulash
- Creamy Pumpkin Mac and Cheese
- Macaroni and Cheese Stuffed Peppers
- Mediterranean Macaroni Salad
- Chicken Bacon Ranch Mac and Cheese
- Macaroni with Creamy Garlic Parmesan Sauce
- Philly Cheesesteak Mac and Cheese
- Chili Macaroni Stuffed Bell Peppers
- Macaroni with Tomato and Basil Sauce
- Ham and Peas Macaroni Alfredo
- Caramelized Onion and Mushroom Mac and Cheese
- Crab Macaroni and Cheese
- Caprese Macaroni Salad
- Southwest Chicken Mac and Cheese
- Macaroni with Spicy Sausage and Tomato Sauce
- Artichoke and Spinach Macaroni Bake
- Jalapeño Popper Mac and Cheese

- Macaroni with Lemon Garlic Butter Sauce
- Pulled Pork Mac and Cheese
- Avocado and Bacon Macaroni Salad
- Baked Ziti Macaroni Casserole
- Chicken Florentine Mac and Cheese
- Macaroni with Smoky Chipotle Cheese Sauce
- Shrimp Scampi Macaroni
- Tomato Basil Pesto Mac and Cheese
- Macaroni with White Wine and Mushroom Sauce
- Italian Sausage and Kale Macaroni Bake

Classic Macaroni and Cheese

Ingredients:

- 8 ounces elbow macaroni
- 1/4 cup unsalted butter
- 1/4 cup all-purpose flour
- 1/2 teaspoon salt
- 1/4 teaspoon black pepper
- 1/4 teaspoon onion powder
- 1/4 teaspoon mustard powder
- 2 1/2 cups whole milk
- 3 cups sharp cheddar cheese, shredded

Instructions:

Cook the elbow macaroni according to the package instructions. Drain and set aside.
In a large saucepan, melt the butter over medium heat.
Stir in the flour, salt, pepper, onion powder, and mustard powder until well combined, creating a roux.
Gradually whisk in the milk, ensuring there are no lumps. Continue cooking and stirring until the mixture thickens, about 5-7 minutes.
Reduce the heat to low and add the shredded cheddar cheese. Stir until the cheese is completely melted and the sauce is smooth.
Add the cooked macaroni to the cheese sauce, stirring until the pasta is evenly coated.
Serve the classic macaroni and cheese immediately, optionally topping with additional shredded cheese or breadcrumbs for extra texture.
Enjoy the creamy and comforting Classic Macaroni and Cheese as a standalone dish or as a side to your favorite main course.

Baked Macaroni with Cheddar and Breadcrumbs

Ingredients:

- 8 ounces elbow macaroni
- 2 tablespoons unsalted butter
- 2 tablespoons all-purpose flour
- 2 cups whole milk
- 2 cups sharp cheddar cheese, shredded
- 1/2 teaspoon Dijon mustard
- Salt and black pepper, to taste
- 1 cup breadcrumbs
- 2 tablespoons melted butter
- Fresh parsley, chopped (for garnish)

Instructions:

Preheat the oven to 350°F (175°C).

Cook the elbow macaroni according to the package instructions. Drain and set aside.

In a large saucepan, melt 2 tablespoons of butter over medium heat. Stir in the flour to create a roux.

Gradually whisk in the milk, ensuring there are no lumps. Continue cooking and stirring until the mixture thickens, about 5-7 minutes.

Add the shredded cheddar cheese and Dijon mustard to the sauce. Stir until the cheese is melted and the sauce is smooth. Season with salt and black pepper to taste.

Add the cooked macaroni to the cheese sauce, stirring until well coated.

Transfer the macaroni and cheese mixture to a greased baking dish.

In a small bowl, combine the breadcrumbs with melted butter. Sprinkle the breadcrumb mixture evenly over the macaroni and cheese.

Bake in the preheated oven for 20-25 minutes or until the top is golden brown and the edges are bubbling.

Remove from the oven and let it cool for a few minutes. Garnish with chopped fresh parsley.

Serve the Baked Macaroni with Cheddar and Breadcrumbs hot, and enjoy the crunchy topping over the creamy macaroni and cheese.

Creamy Alfredo Mac and Cheese

Ingredients:

- 8 ounces elbow macaroni
- 1/2 cup unsalted butter
- 1 cup heavy cream
- 1 cup whole milk
- 2 cups Parmesan cheese, grated
- 2 cups mozzarella cheese, shredded
- 1 teaspoon garlic powder
- Salt and black pepper, to taste
- Fresh parsley, chopped (for garnish)

Instructions:

Cook the elbow macaroni according to the package instructions. Drain and set aside.
In a large saucepan, melt the butter over medium heat.
Pour in the heavy cream and whole milk, stirring to combine.
Gradually add the Parmesan and mozzarella cheeses, stirring continuously until the cheeses are fully melted and the sauce is smooth.
Season the sauce with garlic powder, salt, and black pepper to taste. Stir well.
Add the cooked macaroni to the Alfredo cheese sauce, stirring until the pasta is evenly coated.
Cook for an additional 2-3 minutes, allowing the flavors to meld.
Garnish the Creamy Alfredo Mac and Cheese with chopped fresh parsley.
Serve hot, and savor the luxurious combination of Alfredo sauce and macaroni for a comforting and indulgent meal.

Spicy Buffalo Macaroni and Cheese

Ingredients:

- 8 ounces elbow macaroni
- 1/4 cup unsalted butter
- 1/4 cup all-purpose flour
- 2 cups whole milk
- 2 cups sharp cheddar cheese, shredded
- 1/2 cup blue cheese, crumbled
- 1/2 cup buffalo sauce
- 1 teaspoon garlic powder
- Salt and black pepper, to taste
- 1 cup cooked and shredded chicken (optional)
- Green onions, chopped (for garnish)

Instructions:

Cook the elbow macaroni according to the package instructions. Drain and set aside.

In a large saucepan, melt the butter over medium heat. Stir in the flour to create a roux.

Gradually whisk in the milk, ensuring there are no lumps. Continue cooking and stirring until the mixture thickens, about 5-7 minutes.

Add the shredded cheddar cheese and crumbled blue cheese to the sauce. Stir until the cheeses are melted and the sauce is smooth.

Stir in the buffalo sauce and garlic powder. Season with salt and black pepper to taste.

If using, fold in the cooked and shredded chicken.

Add the cooked macaroni to the spicy buffalo cheese sauce, stirring until well combined.

Cook for an additional 2-3 minutes, allowing the flavors to meld.

Garnish the Spicy Buffalo Macaroni and Cheese with chopped green onions.

Serve hot, and enjoy the bold and zesty flavors of this buffalo-infused mac and cheese with a kick!

Lobster Mac and Cheese

Ingredients:

- 8 ounces elbow macaroni
- 1/4 cup unsalted butter
- 1/4 cup all-purpose flour
- 2 cups whole milk
- 1 cup heavy cream
- 2 cups sharp cheddar cheese, shredded
- 1 cup Gruyere cheese, shredded
- 1/2 cup Parmesan cheese, grated
- 1/2 teaspoon Dijon mustard
- Salt and black pepper, to taste
- 1 1/2 cups cooked lobster meat, chopped
- 1/4 cup fresh chives, chopped (for garnish)
- Breadcrumbs (optional, for topping)

Instructions:

Cook the elbow macaroni according to the package instructions. Drain and set aside.
In a large saucepan, melt the butter over medium heat. Stir in the flour to create a roux.
Gradually whisk in the milk and heavy cream, ensuring there are no lumps.
Continue cooking and stirring until the mixture thickens, about 5-7 minutes.
Add the shredded cheddar, Gruyere, and Parmesan cheeses to the sauce. Stir until the cheeses are melted and the sauce is smooth.
Stir in the Dijon mustard, salt, and black pepper to taste.
Add the cooked macaroni to the cheese sauce, stirring until well coated.
Gently fold in the chopped lobster meat, ensuring it is evenly distributed throughout the mixture.
If desired, sprinkle breadcrumbs over the top for a crispy topping.
Bake in a preheated oven at 375°F (190°C) for 20-25 minutes or until the top is golden brown and the edges are bubbling.
Remove from the oven and let it cool for a few minutes.
Garnish the Lobster Mac and Cheese with chopped fresh chives.
Serve hot, and indulge in the decadent combination of lobster and creamy cheese sauce for a luxurious macaroni experience.

Pesto Cavatappi

Ingredients:

- 8 ounces cavatappi pasta
- 1 cup fresh basil leaves, packed
- 1/2 cup pine nuts, toasted
- 1/2 cup Parmesan cheese, grated
- 2 cloves garlic, peeled
- 1/2 cup extra-virgin olive oil
- Salt and black pepper, to taste
- 1 cup cherry tomatoes, halved
- 1/2 cup mozzarella cheese, diced
- Fresh basil, for garnish

Instructions:

Cook the cavatappi pasta according to the package instructions. Drain and set aside.
In a food processor, combine fresh basil, toasted pine nuts, grated Parmesan cheese, and garlic cloves. Pulse until finely chopped.
With the food processor running, slowly pour in the olive oil until the mixture forms a smooth pesto sauce. Season with salt and black pepper to taste.
In a large mixing bowl, toss the cooked cavatappi pasta with the freshly made pesto sauce until well coated.
Gently fold in the cherry tomatoes and diced mozzarella.
Garnish with fresh basil leaves.
Serve the Pesto Cavatappi warm or at room temperature, and savor the vibrant flavors of this classic pasta dish with a delightful pesto twist.

Tex-Mex Macaroni Casserole

Ingredients:

- 8 ounces elbow macaroni
- 1 pound ground beef
- 1 onion, diced
- 1 bell pepper, diced
- 2 cloves garlic, minced

- 1 can (14 ounces) diced tomatoes, drained
- 1 can (15 ounces) black beans, drained and rinsed
- 1 cup corn kernels (fresh or frozen)
- 1 packet taco seasoning
- 1 cup salsa
- 1 cup shredded cheddar cheese
- 1 cup shredded Monterey Jack cheese
- Sour cream, for serving
- Fresh cilantro, chopped (for garnish)

Instructions:

Cook the elbow macaroni according to the package instructions. Drain and set aside.
Preheat the oven to 350°F (175°C).
In a large skillet, cook the ground beef over medium heat until browned. Drain excess fat.
Add diced onion, bell pepper, and minced garlic to the skillet. Cook until the vegetables are softened.
Stir in diced tomatoes, black beans, corn, and taco seasoning. Cook for an additional 2-3 minutes.
Add the cooked macaroni to the skillet, along with salsa. Stir until well combined.
In a greased baking dish, layer half of the macaroni mixture. Sprinkle half of the shredded cheddar and Monterey Jack cheeses over the layer.
Add the remaining macaroni mixture and top with the remaining shredded cheeses.
Bake in the preheated oven for 20-25 minutes or until the cheese is melted and bubbly.
Remove from the oven and let it cool for a few minutes.
Garnish with chopped fresh cilantro.
Serve the Tex-Mex Macaroni Casserole hot, with a dollop of sour cream on top for an extra burst of flavor. Enjoy the delicious fusion of Tex-Mex and pasta in every bite!

Three-Cheese Macaroni Gratin

Ingredients:

- 8 ounces elbow macaroni
- 1/4 cup unsalted butter
- 1/4 cup all-purpose flour
- 2 cups whole milk
- 1 cup heavy cream
- 1 cup sharp cheddar cheese, shredded
- 1/2 cup Gruyere cheese, shredded
- 1/2 cup Parmesan cheese, grated
- Salt and black pepper, to taste
- 1/4 teaspoon nutmeg (optional)
- 1 cup breadcrumbs
- 2 tablespoons melted butter
- Fresh parsley, chopped (for garnish)

Instructions:

Cook the elbow macaroni according to the package instructions. Drain and set aside.
In a large saucepan, melt the butter over medium heat. Stir in the flour to create a roux.
Gradually whisk in the milk and heavy cream, ensuring there are no lumps.
Continue cooking and stirring until the mixture thickens, about 5-7 minutes.
Add the shredded cheddar, Gruyere, and Parmesan cheeses to the sauce. Stir until the cheeses are melted and the sauce is smooth.
Season the sauce with salt, black pepper, and nutmeg (if using).
Add the cooked macaroni to the cheese sauce, stirring until well coated.
In a small bowl, combine breadcrumbs with melted butter.
Transfer the macaroni and cheese mixture to a greased baking dish.
Sprinkle the breadcrumb mixture evenly over the top.
Bake in a preheated oven at 375°F (190°C) for 20-25 minutes or until the top is golden brown and the edges are bubbling.
Remove from the oven and let it cool for a few minutes.
Garnish with chopped fresh parsley.

Serve the Three-Cheese Macaroni Gratin hot, and revel in the rich and creamy blend of three cheeses with a crispy breadcrumb topping.

Bacon and Jalapeño Mac and Cheese

Ingredients:

- 8 ounces elbow macaroni
- 1/2 pound bacon, cooked and crumbled
- 1/4 cup unsalted butter
- 1/4 cup all-purpose flour
- 2 cups whole milk
- 1 cup heavy cream
- 2 cups sharp cheddar cheese, shredded
- 1 cup Monterey Jack cheese, shredded
- 1/2 cup Parmesan cheese, grated
- Salt and black pepper, to taste
- 2 jalapeños, diced (seeds removed for less heat)
- 1/4 cup breadcrumbs
- 2 tablespoons melted butter
- Fresh cilantro, chopped (for garnish)

Instructions:

Cook the elbow macaroni according to the package instructions. Drain and set aside.
In a large skillet, cook the bacon until crispy. Remove from the skillet, drain excess fat, and crumble the bacon.
In the same skillet, melt the butter over medium heat. Stir in the flour to create a roux.
Gradually whisk in the milk and heavy cream, ensuring there are no lumps.
Continue cooking and stirring until the mixture thickens, about 5-7 minutes.
Add the shredded cheddar, Monterey Jack, and Parmesan cheeses to the sauce.
Stir until the cheeses are melted and the sauce is smooth.
Season the sauce with salt and black pepper to taste.
Add the cooked macaroni to the cheese sauce, stirring until well coated.
Fold in the crumbled bacon and diced jalapeños.
In a small bowl, combine breadcrumbs with melted butter.
Transfer the macaroni and cheese mixture to a greased baking dish.
Sprinkle the breadcrumb mixture evenly over the top.
Broil in the oven for 2-3 minutes or until the breadcrumbs are golden brown.

Remove from the oven and let it cool for a few minutes.
Garnish with chopped fresh cilantro.
Serve the Bacon and Jalapeño Mac and Cheese hot, and experience the delightful combination of smoky bacon, spicy jalapeños, and creamy cheese in every mouthful.

Broccoli and Cheddar Macaroni Bake

Ingredients:

- 8 ounces elbow macaroni
- 2 cups broccoli florets, blanched
- 1/4 cup unsalted butter
- 1/4 cup all-purpose flour
- 2 cups whole milk
- 1 cup heavy cream
- 2 cups sharp cheddar cheese, shredded
- 1/2 cup Parmesan cheese, grated
- Salt and black pepper, to taste
- 1/2 teaspoon Dijon mustard
- 1/4 teaspoon nutmeg
- 1/2 cup breadcrumbs
- 2 tablespoons melted butter
- Fresh parsley, chopped (for garnish)

Instructions:

Cook the elbow macaroni according to the package instructions. Drain and set aside.

Blanch the broccoli florets in boiling water for 2-3 minutes until slightly tender. Drain and set aside.

In a large saucepan, melt the butter over medium heat. Stir in the flour to create a roux.

Gradually whisk in the milk and heavy cream, ensuring there are no lumps.

Continue cooking and stirring until the mixture thickens, about 5-7 minutes.

Add the shredded cheddar and Parmesan cheeses to the sauce. Stir until the cheeses are melted and the sauce is smooth.

Season the sauce with salt, black pepper, Dijon mustard, and nutmeg.

Add the cooked macaroni and blanched broccoli to the cheese sauce, stirring until well coated.

Transfer the macaroni and broccoli mixture to a greased baking dish.

In a small bowl, combine breadcrumbs with melted butter.

Sprinkle the breadcrumb mixture evenly over the top.

Bake in a preheated oven at 375°F (190°C) for 20-25 minutes or until the top is golden brown and the edges are bubbling.

Remove from the oven and let it cool for a few minutes.
Garnish with chopped fresh parsley.
Serve the Broccoli and Cheddar Macaroni Bake hot, and relish the comforting blend of cheesy goodness with the added nutrition of broccoli.

Macaroni Carbonara

Ingredients:

- 8 ounces elbow macaroni
- 1/2 cup pancetta or bacon, diced
- 2 cloves garlic, minced
- 2 large eggs
- 1 cup Parmesan cheese, grated
- Salt and black pepper, to taste
- 1/2 cup fresh parsley, chopped
- Extra Parmesan cheese, for serving

Instructions:

Cook the elbow macaroni according to the package instructions. Drain and set aside.

In a large skillet over medium heat, cook the diced pancetta or bacon until crispy. Add minced garlic and sauté for about 1 minute.

In a bowl, whisk together the eggs and grated Parmesan cheese. Season with salt and black pepper.

Add the cooked macaroni to the skillet with the pancetta and garlic. Toss until well combined.

Remove the skillet from heat, and quickly pour the egg and Parmesan mixture over the macaroni. Toss continuously to coat the pasta evenly and create a creamy sauce.

The heat from the pasta will cook the eggs and create a smooth, creamy sauce. Stir in chopped fresh parsley for added freshness.

Serve the Macaroni Carbonara immediately, with extra Parmesan cheese on the side for those who want an extra cheesy kick.

Enjoy this classic Roman pasta dish with a delightful twist of macaroni!

Chili Mac

Ingredients:

- 8 ounces elbow macaroni
- 1 pound ground beef
- 1 onion, diced
- 2 cloves garlic, minced
- 1 can (14 ounces) diced tomatoes
- 1 can (15 ounces) kidney beans, drained and rinsed
- 1 can (15 ounces) black beans, drained and rinsed
- 1 cup corn kernels (fresh or frozen)
- 1 packet chili seasoning mix
- 1 cup beef broth
- Salt and black pepper, to taste
- 1 cup shredded cheddar cheese
- Green onions, chopped (for garnish)
- Sour cream (optional, for serving)

Instructions:

Cook the elbow macaroni according to the package instructions. Drain and set aside.
In a large skillet over medium heat, brown the ground beef. Add diced onions and minced garlic, and cook until the onions are translucent.
Stir in diced tomatoes, kidney beans, black beans, corn, and chili seasoning mix. Pour in beef broth and season with salt and black pepper.
Simmer the chili mixture for about 10-15 minutes, allowing the flavors to meld and the mixture to thicken.
Add the cooked macaroni to the chili mixture, tossing to combine.
Sprinkle shredded cheddar cheese over the top and let it melt.
Garnish with chopped green onions.
Serve the Chili Mac hot, with a dollop of sour cream if desired.
Enjoy this hearty and flavorful Chili Mac that combines the comfort of macaroni with the bold flavors of chili!

Greek Macaroni Salad

Ingredients:

- 8 ounces elbow macaroni
- 1 cup cherry tomatoes, halved
- 1 cucumber, diced
- 1/2 red onion, finely chopped
- 1/2 cup Kalamata olives, sliced
- 1/2 cup crumbled feta cheese
- 1/4 cup fresh parsley, chopped
- 1/4 cup fresh mint, chopped
- 1/3 cup extra virgin olive oil
- 2 tablespoons red wine vinegar
- 1 teaspoon Dijon mustard
- 1 clove garlic, minced
- Salt and black pepper, to taste

Instructions:

Cook the elbow macaroni according to the package instructions. Drain and let it cool.

In a large bowl, combine the cooled macaroni with cherry tomatoes, cucumber, red onion, Kalamata olives, feta cheese, parsley, and mint.

In a small bowl, whisk together olive oil, red wine vinegar, Dijon mustard, minced garlic, salt, and black pepper to create the dressing.

Pour the dressing over the macaroni mixture and toss everything together until well coated.

Chill the Greek Macaroni Salad in the refrigerator for at least 30 minutes to allow the flavors to meld.

Before serving, give the salad a gentle toss and adjust the seasoning if necessary.

Serve this refreshing and Mediterranean-inspired Greek Macaroni Salad as a side dish or enjoy it on its own!

Share this flavorful salad with family and friends for a taste of Greece in every bite.

Sundried Tomato and Feta Macaroni

Ingredients:

- 8 ounces elbow macaroni
- 1/2 cup sundried tomatoes, chopped
- 1/2 cup crumbled feta cheese
- 1/4 cup fresh basil, chopped
- 1/4 cup fresh parsley, chopped
- 1/4 cup pine nuts, toasted
- 1/3 cup extra virgin olive oil
- 2 tablespoons balsamic vinegar
- 1 clove garlic, minced
- Salt and black pepper, to taste
- Red pepper flakes (optional, for heat)

Instructions:

Cook the elbow macaroni according to the package instructions. Drain and let it cool.
In a large bowl, combine the cooled macaroni with sundried tomatoes, feta cheese, fresh basil, fresh parsley, and toasted pine nuts.
In a small bowl, whisk together olive oil, balsamic vinegar, minced garlic, salt, and black pepper to create the dressing.
Pour the dressing over the macaroni mixture and toss everything together until well coated.
If you like a bit of heat, sprinkle red pepper flakes over the salad.
Chill the Sundried Tomato and Feta Macaroni in the refrigerator for at least 30 minutes to allow the flavors to meld.
Before serving, give the salad a gentle toss and adjust the seasoning if necessary.
Serve this vibrant and Mediterranean-inspired macaroni dish as a delightful side or enjoy it as a light meal.
Share this flavorful creation with friends and family for a taste of sunny Mediterranean flavors.

Truffle Mac and Cheese

Ingredients:

- 8 ounces elbow macaroni
- 1/4 cup unsalted butter
- 1/4 cup all-purpose flour
- 2 cups whole milk
- 1 cup heavy cream
- 2 cups sharp cheddar cheese, shredded
- 1 cup Gruyère cheese, shredded
- 1/2 cup Parmesan cheese, grated
- Salt and white pepper, to taste
- 1 tablespoon truffle oil
- 1/2 cup panko breadcrumbs
- Fresh chives, chopped (for garnish)

Instructions:

Cook the elbow macaroni according to the package instructions. Drain and set aside.
In a large saucepan, melt the butter over medium heat. Stir in the flour to create a roux.
Gradually whisk in the milk and heavy cream, ensuring there are no lumps.
Continue cooking and stirring until the mixture thickens, about 5-7 minutes.
Add the shredded cheddar, Gruyère, and Parmesan cheeses to the sauce. Stir until the cheeses are melted and the sauce is smooth.
Season the sauce with salt and white pepper to taste.
Add the cooked macaroni to the cheese sauce, stirring until well coated.
Stir in truffle oil, ensuring it is evenly distributed throughout the macaroni and cheese.
In a separate pan, toast panko breadcrumbs until golden brown.
Sprinkle toasted panko breadcrumbs over the top of the macaroni and cheese.
Garnish with chopped fresh chives.
Serve the Truffle Mac and Cheese hot, and savor the luxurious combination of creamy cheese sauce and the earthy aroma of truffle oil.
Share this gourmet mac and cheese with truffle lovers for a decadent dining experience.

Macaroni with Roasted Red Pepper Sauce

Ingredients:

- 8 ounces elbow macaroni
- 2 large red bell peppers, roasted and peeled
- 1/2 cup cherry tomatoes
- 2 cloves garlic, minced
- 1/4 cup extra virgin olive oil
- 1/4 cup grated Parmesan cheese
- 1/4 cup fresh basil, chopped
- Salt and black pepper, to taste
- Crushed red pepper flakes (optional, for heat)
- 1/4 cup pine nuts, toasted (for garnish)

Instructions:

Cook the elbow macaroni according to the package instructions. Drain and set aside.

Preheat the oven broiler. Place red bell peppers on a baking sheet and broil, turning occasionally, until the skin is charred and blistered. Remove from the oven and let them cool. Peel off the skin, remove seeds, and chop the roasted peppers.

In a blender or food processor, combine the roasted red peppers, cherry tomatoes, minced garlic, olive oil, Parmesan cheese, and fresh basil. Blend until smooth.

Season the roasted red pepper sauce with salt and black pepper. Add crushed red pepper flakes if you desire some heat.

In a large pan, heat the red pepper sauce over medium heat.

Add the cooked macaroni to the pan, tossing to coat the pasta evenly with the sauce.

Toast pine nuts in a dry pan until golden brown.

Serve the Macaroni with Roasted Red Pepper Sauce hot, garnished with toasted pine nuts.

Enjoy this vibrant and flavorful macaroni dish with the sweetness of roasted red peppers and the richness of Parmesan cheese.

Spinach and Artichoke Macaroni Casserole

Ingredients:

- 8 ounces elbow macaroni
- 1 tablespoon olive oil
- 1 small onion, finely chopped
- 2 cloves garlic, minced
- 1 can (14 ounces) artichoke hearts, drained and chopped
- 2 cups fresh spinach, chopped
- 1 cup ricotta cheese
- 1 cup mozzarella cheese, shredded
- 1/2 cup Parmesan cheese, grated
- 1/2 cup mayonnaise
- 1/2 cup sour cream
- Salt and black pepper, to taste
- 1/2 teaspoon red pepper flakes (optional, for heat)
- 1/4 cup breadcrumbs
- Fresh parsley, chopped (for garnish)

Instructions:

Cook the elbow macaroni according to the package instructions. Drain and set aside.

Preheat the oven to 375°F (190°C).

In a large skillet, heat olive oil over medium heat. Add chopped onion and sauté until translucent. Add minced garlic and cook for an additional minute.

Stir in chopped artichoke hearts and fresh spinach. Cook until the spinach wilts.

In a large mixing bowl, combine ricotta cheese, mozzarella cheese, Parmesan cheese, mayonnaise, and sour cream. Mix well.

Add the cooked macaroni to the cheese mixture, followed by the sautéed vegetables. Season with salt, black pepper, and red pepper flakes (if using). Mix until everything is well combined.

Transfer the macaroni mixture to a greased casserole dish.

Sprinkle breadcrumbs evenly over the top.

Bake in the preheated oven for 25-30 minutes or until the casserole is bubbly and the top is golden brown.

Garnish with chopped fresh parsley before serving.

Serve this creamy and comforting Spinach and Artichoke Macaroni Casserole as a delicious main dish or side.

Share this flavorful casserole with friends and family for a satisfying meal with a hint of spinach and artichoke goodness!

Taco Macaroni Skillet

Ingredients:

- 8 ounces elbow macaroni
- 1 pound ground beef
- 1 small onion, finely chopped
- 1 packet taco seasoning
- 1 can (14 ounces) diced tomatoes, undrained
- 1 can (4 ounces) diced green chilies
- 1 can (15 ounces) black beans, drained and rinsed
- 1 cup corn kernels (fresh or frozen)
- 1 cup shredded cheddar cheese
- 1/2 cup sour cream
- Fresh cilantro, chopped (for garnish)
- Avocado slices (for garnish)
- Lime wedges (for serving)

Instructions:

Cook the elbow macaroni according to the package instructions. Drain and set aside.

In a large skillet over medium heat, brown the ground beef. Drain any excess fat.

Add chopped onion to the skillet and cook until the onion is soft.

Stir in the taco seasoning, diced tomatoes (with juices), diced green chilies, black beans, and corn. Simmer for about 5 minutes until heated through.

Add the cooked macaroni to the skillet, mixing well with the taco meat and vegetables.

Sprinkle shredded cheddar cheese over the top and cover the skillet. Allow the cheese to melt.

Once the cheese is melted, remove the skillet from heat.

Dollop sour cream over the macaroni mixture.

Garnish with chopped cilantro and serve with avocado slices and lime wedges on the side.

Serve this Taco Macaroni Skillet hot, allowing everyone to customize their servings with their favorite toppings.

Enjoy the fusion of taco flavors and comforting macaroni in this easy and satisfying skillet dish!

Macaroni Goulash

Ingredients:

- 8 ounces elbow macaroni
- 1 pound ground beef
- 1 onion, finely chopped
- 2 cloves garlic, minced
- 1 can (15 ounces) tomato sauce
- 1 can (14 ounces) diced tomatoes, undrained
- 1 cup beef broth
- 1 teaspoon paprika
- 1/2 teaspoon caraway seeds
- Salt and black pepper, to taste
- 1 cup frozen peas
- 1 cup corn kernels (fresh or frozen)
- Chopped fresh parsley (for garnish)

Instructions:

Cook the elbow macaroni according to the package instructions. Drain and set aside.
In a large skillet over medium heat, brown the ground beef. Drain any excess fat.
Add chopped onion to the skillet and cook until the onion is soft.
Stir in minced garlic and cook for an additional minute until fragrant.
Add tomato sauce, diced tomatoes (with juices), beef broth, paprika, caraway seeds, salt, and black pepper to the skillet. Bring the mixture to a simmer.
Add frozen peas and corn to the skillet, stirring well. Simmer for about 5-7 minutes until the vegetables are heated through.
Add the cooked macaroni to the skillet, mixing it with the goulash until well combined.
Simmer for an additional 5 minutes to allow the flavors to meld.
Adjust seasoning if necessary.
Garnish with chopped fresh parsley before serving.
Serve this hearty and flavorful Macaroni Goulash hot, and enjoy the comforting blend of pasta, seasoned ground beef, and vegetables.
Share this satisfying goulash with friends and family for a wholesome meal!

Creamy Pumpkin Mac and Cheese

Ingredients:

- 8 ounces elbow macaroni
- 2 tablespoons unsalted butter
- 1/4 cup all-purpose flour
- 2 cups whole milk
- 1 cup canned pumpkin puree
- 2 cups sharp cheddar cheese, shredded
- 1 cup Gruyère cheese, shredded
- 1/2 cup Parmesan cheese, grated
- 1/2 teaspoon ground nutmeg
- Salt and black pepper, to taste
- 1/4 cup breadcrumbs
- Fresh sage leaves, chopped (for garnish)

Instructions:

Cook the elbow macaroni according to the package instructions. Drain and set aside.

In a large saucepan, melt the butter over medium heat. Stir in the flour to create a roux.

Gradually whisk in the milk, ensuring there are no lumps. Continue cooking and stirring until the mixture thickens, about 5-7 minutes.

Add pumpkin puree, shredded cheddar, Gruyère, and Parmesan cheeses to the sauce. Stir until the cheeses are melted and the sauce is smooth.

Season the sauce with ground nutmeg, salt, and black pepper to taste.

Add the cooked macaroni to the sauce, tossing to coat the pasta evenly with the creamy pumpkin mixture.

Preheat the oven broiler.

Transfer the pumpkin mac and cheese to an oven-safe dish.

Sprinkle breadcrumbs evenly over the top.

Place the dish under the broiler for 2-3 minutes or until the breadcrumbs are golden brown.

Garnish with chopped fresh sage leaves before serving.

Serve this Creamy Pumpkin Mac and Cheese hot, and savor the comforting combination of pumpkin and rich, cheesy goodness.

Enjoy this seasonal twist on classic mac and cheese for a cozy and delicious meal!

Macaroni and Cheese Stuffed Peppers

Ingredients:

- 4 large bell peppers, halved and seeds removed
- 8 ounces elbow macaroni
- 2 tablespoons unsalted butter
- 2 tablespoons all-purpose flour
- 2 cups whole milk
- 2 cups sharp cheddar cheese, shredded
- 1 cup Gruyère cheese, shredded
- 1/2 cup Parmesan cheese, grated
- Salt and black pepper, to taste
- 1/4 cup breadcrumbs
- Chopped fresh parsley (for garnish)

Instructions:

Preheat the oven to 375°F (190°C).
Cook the elbow macaroni according to the package instructions. Drain and set aside.
In a large saucepan, melt the butter over medium heat. Stir in the flour to create a roux.
Gradually whisk in the milk, ensuring there are no lumps. Continue cooking and stirring until the mixture thickens, about 5-7 minutes.
Add shredded cheddar, Gruyère, and Parmesan cheeses to the sauce. Stir until the cheeses are melted and the sauce is smooth.
Season the sauce with salt and black pepper to taste.
Add the cooked macaroni to the sauce, tossing to coat the pasta evenly with the cheesy mixture.
Arrange the halved bell peppers in a baking dish.
Spoon the macaroni and cheese mixture into each pepper half.
Sprinkle breadcrumbs evenly over the top.
Bake in the preheated oven for 20-25 minutes or until the peppers are tender.
Garnish with chopped fresh parsley before serving.
Serve these Macaroni and Cheese Stuffed Peppers hot, and enjoy the delightful combination of cheesy macaroni inside colorful bell peppers.
Share this unique and delicious dish as a creative twist on stuffed peppers!

Mediterranean Macaroni Salad

Ingredients:

- 8 ounces elbow macaroni
- 1/4 cup extra-virgin olive oil
- 3 tablespoons red wine vinegar
- 2 cloves garlic, minced
- 1 teaspoon Dijon mustard
- 1 teaspoon dried oregano
- Salt and black pepper, to taste
- 1 cup cherry tomatoes, halved
- 1 cucumber, diced
- 1/2 cup Kalamata olives, sliced
- 1/2 cup red onion, finely chopped
- 1/2 cup crumbled feta cheese
- Fresh parsley, chopped (for garnish)
- Lemon wedges (for serving)

Instructions:

Cook the elbow macaroni according to the package instructions. Drain and let it cool.
In a large bowl, whisk together olive oil, red wine vinegar, minced garlic, Dijon mustard, dried oregano, salt, and black pepper to create the dressing.
Add the cooled macaroni to the dressing, tossing to coat the pasta evenly.
Gently fold in cherry tomatoes, diced cucumber, sliced Kalamata olives, chopped red onion, and crumbled feta cheese.
Adjust salt and pepper to taste.
Chill the Mediterranean Macaroni Salad in the refrigerator for at least 1 hour to allow the flavors to meld.
Before serving, garnish with chopped fresh parsley and serve with lemon wedges on the side.
Serve this refreshing and vibrant Mediterranean Macaroni Salad as a delightful side dish or a light meal.
Enjoy the Mediterranean-inspired flavors and the combination of textures in this delicious pasta salad!

Chicken Bacon Ranch Mac and Cheese

Ingredients:

- 8 ounces elbow macaroni
- 1 tablespoon olive oil
- 1 pound boneless, skinless chicken breasts, diced
- Salt and black pepper, to taste
- 6 slices bacon, cooked and crumbled
- 1/4 cup unsalted butter
- 1/4 cup all-purpose flour
- 2 cups whole milk
- 2 cups shredded sharp cheddar cheese
- 1 cup shredded mozzarella cheese
- 1/2 cup grated Parmesan cheese
- 1 packet ranch seasoning mix
- 1/2 teaspoon garlic powder
- 1/2 teaspoon onion powder
- Fresh chives, chopped (for garnish)

Instructions:

Cook the elbow macaroni according to the package instructions. Drain and set aside.

In a large skillet, heat olive oil over medium-high heat. Season diced chicken with salt and black pepper, then cook in the skillet until browned and cooked through. Remove from the skillet and set aside.

In the same skillet, add the crumbled bacon and cook until crisp. Remove from the skillet and set aside.

In a large pot, melt the butter over medium heat. Stir in the flour to create a roux. Gradually whisk in the milk, ensuring there are no lumps. Continue cooking and stirring until the mixture thickens, about 5-7 minutes.

Add shredded cheddar, mozzarella, and Parmesan cheeses to the pot. Stir until the cheeses are melted and the sauce is smooth.

Season the sauce with ranch seasoning mix, garlic powder, and onion powder. Adjust salt and black pepper to taste.

Add the cooked macaroni, diced chicken, and crumbled bacon to the cheese sauce, tossing to coat everything evenly.

Serve the Chicken Bacon Ranch Mac and Cheese hot, garnished with fresh chopped chives.

Enjoy this indulgent and flavorful twist on classic mac and cheese with the delicious combination of chicken, bacon, and ranch!

Macaroni with Creamy Garlic Parmesan Sauce

Ingredients:

- 8 ounces elbow macaroni
- 2 tablespoons unsalted butter
- 4 cloves garlic, minced
- 2 tablespoons all-purpose flour
- 2 cups whole milk
- 1 cup grated Parmesan cheese
- 1 cup shredded mozzarella cheese
- Salt and black pepper, to taste
- 1/2 teaspoon dried Italian herbs (optional)
- Fresh parsley, chopped (for garnish)

Instructions:

Cook the elbow macaroni according to the package instructions. Drain and set aside.

In a large saucepan, melt the butter over medium heat. Add minced garlic and sauté for about 1 minute until fragrant.

Stir in the flour to create a roux. Cook for an additional 1-2 minutes to eliminate the raw flour taste.

Gradually whisk in the milk, ensuring there are no lumps. Continue cooking and stirring until the mixture thickens, about 5-7 minutes.

Add grated Parmesan and shredded mozzarella cheeses to the sauce. Stir until the cheeses are melted and the sauce is smooth.

Season the sauce with salt and black pepper to taste. Add dried Italian herbs if desired.

Add the cooked macaroni to the sauce, tossing to coat the pasta evenly with the creamy garlic Parmesan mixture.

Serve the Macaroni with Creamy Garlic Parmesan Sauce hot, garnished with fresh chopped parsley.

Enjoy this rich and flavorful macaroni dish that features a luxurious blend of creamy garlic Parmesan goodness!

Philly Cheesesteak Mac and Cheese

Ingredients:

- 8 ounces elbow macaroni
- 1 tablespoon olive oil
- 1 pound beef sirloin or ribeye steak, thinly sliced
- Salt and black pepper, to taste
- 1 onion, thinly sliced
- 1 bell pepper, thinly sliced
- 2 tablespoons unsalted butter
- 2 tablespoons all-purpose flour
- 2 cups whole milk
- 2 cups shredded provolone cheese
- 1 cup shredded white cheddar cheese
- 1/2 cup grated Parmesan cheese
- Salt and black pepper, to taste
- 1 teaspoon Worcestershire sauce
- 1 teaspoon Dijon mustard
- 8 slices provolone cheese (for topping)

Instructions:

Cook the elbow macaroni according to the package instructions. Drain and set aside.

In a large skillet, heat olive oil over medium-high heat. Season the thinly sliced beef with salt and black pepper, then cook in the skillet until browned. Remove from the skillet and set aside.

In the same skillet, add sliced onion and bell pepper. Cook until the vegetables are softened. Remove from the skillet and set aside.

In a large pot, melt the butter over medium heat. Stir in the flour to create a roux. Gradually whisk in the milk, ensuring there are no lumps. Continue cooking and stirring until the mixture thickens, about 5-7 minutes.

Add shredded provolone, white cheddar, and Parmesan cheeses to the pot. Stir until the cheeses are melted and the sauce is smooth.

Season the sauce with salt, black pepper, Worcestershire sauce, and Dijon mustard.

Add the cooked macaroni, cooked beef, and sautéed vegetables to the cheese sauce, tossing to coat everything evenly.

Preheat the oven broiler.

Transfer the Philly Cheesesteak Mac and Cheese to an oven-safe dish. Top with slices of provolone cheese.

Place the dish under the broiler for 2-3 minutes or until the cheese is melted and bubbly.

Serve this indulgent and savory Philly Cheesesteak Mac and Cheese hot, and savor the flavors reminiscent of the iconic sandwich!

Enjoy the fusion of two classic comfort foods in one delicious dish.

Chili Macaroni Stuffed Bell Peppers

Ingredients:

- 4 large bell peppers, halved and seeds removed
- 8 ounces elbow macaroni
- 1 pound ground beef
- 1 onion, diced
- 2 cloves garlic, minced
- 1 can (15 ounces) kidney beans, drained and rinsed
- 1 can (15 ounces) diced tomatoes, undrained
- 1 can (6 ounces) tomato paste
- 2 tablespoons chili powder
- 1 teaspoon cumin
- 1 teaspoon paprika
- Salt and black pepper, to taste
- 1 cup shredded cheddar cheese
- Fresh cilantro, chopped (for garnish)
- Sour cream (optional, for serving)

Instructions:

Preheat the oven to 375°F (190°C).
Cook the elbow macaroni according to the package instructions. Drain and set aside.
In a large skillet, cook the ground beef over medium heat until browned. Drain excess fat.
Add diced onion and minced garlic to the skillet. Cook until the onion is softened.
Stir in kidney beans, diced tomatoes, tomato paste, chili powder, cumin, paprika, salt, and black pepper. Let it simmer for about 10 minutes.
Add the cooked macaroni to the beef and chili mixture, stirring to combine.
Arrange the bell pepper halves in a baking dish.
Spoon the chili macaroni mixture into each pepper half.
Top each stuffed pepper with shredded cheddar cheese.
Bake in the preheated oven for 20-25 minutes or until the peppers are tender, and the cheese is melted and bubbly.
Garnish with chopped fresh cilantro and serve with optional sour cream on the side.

Enjoy these Chili Macaroni Stuffed Bell Peppers as a hearty and flavorful meal that combines the comfort of chili mac with the fun twist of stuffed peppers!

Macaroni with Tomato and Basil Sauce

Ingredients:

- 8 ounces elbow macaroni
- 2 tablespoons olive oil
- 4 cloves garlic, minced
- 1 can (28 ounces) crushed tomatoes
- 1 teaspoon dried oregano
- 1 teaspoon dried basil
- 1/2 teaspoon red pepper flakes (optional)
- Salt and black pepper, to taste
- 1/4 cup fresh basil, chopped
- Grated Parmesan cheese, for serving

Instructions:

Cook the elbow macaroni according to the package instructions. Drain and set aside.
In a large saucepan, heat olive oil over medium heat. Add minced garlic and sauté for about 1 minute until fragrant.
Pour in the crushed tomatoes and add dried oregano, dried basil, red pepper flakes (if using), salt, and black pepper. Stir to combine.
Simmer the sauce over medium-low heat for 15-20 minutes, allowing the flavors to meld and the sauce to thicken.
Add the cooked macaroni to the tomato and basil sauce, tossing to coat the pasta evenly.
Stir in fresh chopped basil just before serving.
Serve the Macaroni with Tomato and Basil Sauce hot, garnished with grated Parmesan cheese.
Enjoy this simple and flavorful pasta dish that highlights the classic combination of tomatoes and basil!

Ham and Peas Macaroni Alfredo

Ingredients:

- 8 ounces elbow macaroni
- 2 tablespoons unsalted butter
- 1 cup cooked ham, diced
- 1 cup frozen peas, thawed
- 2 cloves garlic, minced
- 1 cup heavy cream
- 1 cup grated Parmesan cheese
- Salt and black pepper, to taste
- Fresh parsley, chopped (for garnish)

Instructions:

Cook the elbow macaroni according to the package instructions. Drain and set aside.
In a large skillet, melt the butter over medium heat.
Add diced ham to the skillet and sauté until lightly browned.
Stir in minced garlic and cook for about 1 minute until fragrant.
Add thawed peas to the skillet and cook for an additional 2 minutes.
Pour in the heavy cream and bring the mixture to a simmer.
Stir in grated Parmesan cheese, salt, and black pepper. Continue stirring until the cheese is melted and the sauce is smooth.
Add the cooked macaroni to the skillet, tossing to coat the pasta evenly with the creamy Alfredo sauce.
Serve the Ham and Peas Macaroni Alfredo hot, garnished with chopped fresh parsley.
Enjoy this comforting and flavorful pasta dish that combines the richness of Alfredo sauce with the delightful addition of ham and peas!

Caramelized Onion and Mushroom Mac and Cheese

Ingredients:

- 8 ounces elbow macaroni
- 2 tablespoons unsalted butter
- 1 large onion, thinly sliced
- 8 ounces mushrooms, sliced
- 2 cloves garlic, minced
- 2 tablespoons all-purpose flour
- 2 cups whole milk
- 2 cups shredded sharp cheddar cheese
- Salt and black pepper, to taste
- 1/4 teaspoon nutmeg (optional)
- 1/2 cup breadcrumbs
- Fresh parsley, chopped (for garnish)

Instructions:

Cook the elbow macaroni according to the package instructions. Drain and set aside.
In a large skillet, melt the butter over medium heat.
Add sliced onions to the skillet and cook over medium-low heat, stirring occasionally, until caramelized, about 15-20 minutes.
Add sliced mushrooms and minced garlic to the skillet. Cook until the mushrooms are tender.
Sprinkle flour over the onion and mushroom mixture. Stir well to combine.
Gradually whisk in the milk, ensuring there are no lumps. Cook and stir until the mixture thickens, about 5-7 minutes.
Add shredded cheddar cheese to the skillet, stirring until the cheese is melted and the sauce is smooth.
Season the sauce with salt, black pepper, and nutmeg (if using).
Add the cooked macaroni to the skillet, tossing to coat the pasta evenly with the creamy onion and mushroom sauce.
Preheat the oven broiler.
Transfer the macaroni and cheese mixture to an oven-safe dish.
Sprinkle breadcrumbs over the top and place under the broiler for 2-3 minutes or until the breadcrumbs are golden brown.

Garnish with chopped fresh parsley and serve the Caramelized Onion and Mushroom Mac and Cheese hot.

Enjoy this sophisticated twist on classic mac and cheese, featuring the rich flavors of caramelized onions and mushrooms!

Crab Macaroni and Cheese

Ingredients:

- 8 ounces elbow macaroni
- 2 tablespoons unsalted butter
- 2 tablespoons all-purpose flour
- 2 cups whole milk
- 2 cups shredded sharp cheddar cheese
- 1 cup shredded Gruyère cheese
- Salt and black pepper, to taste
- 1/4 teaspoon cayenne pepper
- 1/2 cup lump crabmeat, picked over for shells
- 1 tablespoon Dijon mustard
- 1/4 cup breadcrumbs
- Fresh parsley, chopped (for garnish)
- Lemon wedges (for serving)

Instructions:

Cook the elbow macaroni according to the package instructions. Drain and set aside.
In a large saucepan, melt the butter over medium heat.
Sprinkle flour over the melted butter and whisk to create a roux. Cook for 1-2 minutes.
Gradually whisk in the milk, ensuring there are no lumps. Cook and stir until the mixture thickens, about 5-7 minutes.
Add shredded cheddar cheese and Gruyère cheese to the sauce, stirring until the cheeses are melted and the sauce is smooth.
Season the sauce with salt, black pepper, and cayenne pepper.
Stir in lump crabmeat and Dijon mustard until well combined.
Add the cooked macaroni to the cheese and crab mixture, tossing to coat the pasta evenly.
Preheat the oven broiler.
Transfer the Crab Macaroni and Cheese to an oven-safe dish.
Sprinkle breadcrumbs over the top and place under the broiler for 2-3 minutes or until the breadcrumbs are golden brown.
Garnish with chopped fresh parsley and serve hot with lemon wedges on the side.

Enjoy this decadent and indulgent Crab Macaroni and Cheese, featuring the delicate flavor of lump crabmeat!

Caprese Macaroni Salad

Ingredients:

- 8 ounces elbow macaroni
- 1 cup cherry tomatoes, halved
- 1 cup fresh mozzarella balls, halved
- 1/4 cup fresh basil, chopped
- 3 tablespoons extra-virgin olive oil
- 2 tablespoons balsamic vinegar
- Salt and black pepper, to taste
- 1/4 cup grated Parmesan cheese
- Balsamic glaze (for drizzling, optional)

Instructions:

Cook the elbow macaroni according to the package instructions. Drain and set aside to cool.
In a large bowl, combine the cooked macaroni, cherry tomatoes, fresh mozzarella, and chopped basil.
In a small bowl, whisk together the extra-virgin olive oil and balsamic vinegar. Season with salt and black pepper to taste.
Pour the dressing over the macaroni mixture and toss gently to coat all the ingredients.
Add grated Parmesan cheese to the salad and toss again to combine.
Drizzle with balsamic glaze if desired, for an extra burst of flavor.
Refrigerate the Caprese Macaroni Salad for at least 30 minutes to allow the flavors to meld.
Before serving, give the salad a gentle toss and adjust the seasoning if needed.
Serve this refreshing and vibrant Caprese Macaroni Salad as a delightful side dish or a light meal.
Enjoy the classic Caprese flavors combined with the comfort of macaroni in this easy and delicious salad!

Southwest Chicken Mac and Cheese

Ingredients:

- 8 ounces elbow macaroni
- 1 tablespoon olive oil
- 1 pound boneless, skinless chicken breasts, diced
- 1 teaspoon chili powder
- 1 teaspoon cumin
- 1/2 teaspoon smoked paprika
- Salt and black pepper, to taste
- 2 tablespoons unsalted butter
- 2 tablespoons all-purpose flour
- 2 cups whole milk
- 2 cups shredded sharp cheddar cheese
- 1 cup black beans, drained and rinsed
- 1 cup corn kernels (fresh, frozen, or canned)
- 1/4 cup chopped fresh cilantro
- Sliced jalapeños (optional, for garnish)

Instructions:

Cook the elbow macaroni according to the package instructions. Drain and set aside.

In a large skillet, heat olive oil over medium-high heat.

Season diced chicken with chili powder, cumin, smoked paprika, salt, and black pepper.

Add the seasoned chicken to the skillet and cook until browned and cooked through. Set aside.

In a large saucepan, melt the butter over medium heat.

Sprinkle flour over the melted butter and whisk to create a roux. Cook for 1-2 minutes.

Gradually whisk in the milk, ensuring there are no lumps. Cook and stir until the mixture thickens, about 5-7 minutes.

Add shredded cheddar cheese to the sauce, stirring until the cheese is melted and the sauce is smooth.

Season the sauce with salt and black pepper.

Stir in the cooked macaroni, sautéed chicken, black beans, corn, and chopped cilantro. Mix until well combined.
Garnish with sliced jalapeños if desired.
Serve the Southwest Chicken Mac and Cheese hot, and enjoy the bold and flavorful combination of southwest-inspired ingredients!

Macaroni with Spicy Sausage and Tomato Sauce

Ingredients:

- 8 ounces elbow macaroni
- 1 tablespoon olive oil
- 1 pound spicy Italian sausage, casings removed
- 1 onion, finely chopped
- 2 cloves garlic, minced
- 1 can (14 ounces) crushed tomatoes
- 1 can (8 ounces) tomato sauce
- 1 teaspoon dried oregano
- 1 teaspoon dried basil
- 1/2 teaspoon red pepper flakes (adjust to taste)
- Salt and black pepper, to taste
- Grated Parmesan cheese (for serving)
- Fresh basil, chopped (for garnish)

Instructions:

Cook the elbow macaroni according to the package instructions. Drain and set aside.
In a large skillet, heat olive oil over medium-high heat.
Add the spicy Italian sausage to the skillet, breaking it apart with a spoon, and cook until browned.
Add chopped onion and minced garlic to the skillet. Cook until the onion is softened.
Stir in crushed tomatoes, tomato sauce, dried oregano, dried basil, and red pepper flakes. Bring the mixture to a simmer.
Season with salt and black pepper to taste. Reduce heat and let the sauce simmer for about 15-20 minutes, allowing the flavors to meld.
Add the cooked macaroni to the skillet, tossing to coat the pasta evenly with the spicy sausage and tomato sauce.
Serve the Macaroni with Spicy Sausage and Tomato Sauce hot.
Garnish with grated Parmesan cheese and chopped fresh basil.
Enjoy this hearty and flavorful pasta dish that combines the robust taste of spicy sausage with a rich tomato sauce!

Artichoke and Spinach Macaroni Bake

Ingredients:

- 8 ounces elbow macaroni
- 1 tablespoon olive oil
- 1 onion, finely chopped
- 2 cloves garlic, minced
- 1 can (14 ounces) artichoke hearts, drained and chopped
- 1 package (10 ounces) frozen chopped spinach, thawed and drained
- 1 cup ricotta cheese
- 1 cup shredded mozzarella cheese
- 1/2 cup grated Parmesan cheese
- 1 teaspoon dried oregano
- Salt and black pepper, to taste
- 1 can (14 ounces) diced tomatoes, drained
- Fresh basil, chopped (for garnish)

Instructions:

Cook the elbow macaroni according to the package instructions. Drain and set aside.
Preheat the oven to 375°F (190°C).
In a large skillet, heat olive oil over medium heat.
Add chopped onion and minced garlic to the skillet. Cook until the onion is softened.
Stir in chopped artichoke hearts and thawed, drained spinach. Cook for 2-3 minutes.
In a large bowl, combine ricotta cheese, shredded mozzarella cheese, grated Parmesan cheese, dried oregano, salt, and black pepper.
Add the cooked macaroni to the cheese mixture and toss to coat.
Fold in the artichoke and spinach mixture.
Gently stir in diced tomatoes.
Transfer the mixture to a greased baking dish.
Bake in the preheated oven for 20-25 minutes or until the top is golden and bubbly.
Remove from the oven and let it cool for a few minutes.
Garnish with chopped fresh basil.

Serve the Artichoke and Spinach Macaroni Bake warm, and enjoy this delicious and comforting baked pasta dish!

Jalapeño Popper Mac and Cheese

Ingredients:

- 8 ounces elbow macaroni
- 1 tablespoon butter
- 2 tablespoons all-purpose flour
- 2 cups milk
- 2 cups shredded sharp cheddar cheese
- 1 cup shredded mozzarella cheese
- 1/2 cup cream cheese
- Salt and black pepper, to taste
- 1 cup diced jalapeños (fresh or pickled)
- 1 cup breadcrumbs
- 4 slices bacon, cooked and crumbled (optional)
- Chopped fresh cilantro (for garnish)

Instructions:

Cook the elbow macaroni according to the package instructions. Drain and set aside.
In a large saucepan, melt butter over medium heat.
Sprinkle flour over the melted butter and whisk to create a roux. Cook for 1-2 minutes.
Gradually whisk in the milk, ensuring there are no lumps. Cook and stir until the mixture thickens, about 5-7 minutes.
Add shredded sharp cheddar cheese, shredded mozzarella cheese, and cream cheese to the sauce. Stir until the cheeses are melted and the sauce is smooth.
Season the sauce with salt and black pepper to taste.
Stir in diced jalapeños, reserving a few for garnish.
Add the cooked macaroni to the cheese sauce, tossing to coat.
In a separate pan, toast the breadcrumbs until golden brown.
Transfer the macaroni and cheese mixture to a serving dish.
Top with toasted breadcrumbs, crumbled bacon (if using), reserved diced jalapeños, and chopped fresh cilantro.
Serve the Jalapeño Popper Mac and Cheese hot

Macaroni with Lemon Garlic Butter Sauce

Ingredients:

- 8 ounces elbow macaroni
- 3 tablespoons unsalted butter
- 3 cloves garlic, minced
- Zest of 1 lemon
- Juice of 1 lemon
- 1/2 cup grated Parmesan cheese
- Salt and black pepper, to taste
- Fresh parsley, chopped (for garnish)

Instructions:

Cook the elbow macaroni according to the package instructions. Drain and set aside.
In a large skillet, melt the unsalted butter over medium heat.
Add minced garlic to the skillet and sauté for 1-2 minutes until fragrant.
Stir in the lemon zest and lemon juice, combining well.
Add the cooked macaroni to the skillet, tossing to coat in the lemon garlic butter sauce.
Sprinkle grated Parmesan cheese over the macaroni and continue to toss until the cheese is melted.
Season with salt and black pepper to taste.
Transfer the Macaroni with Lemon Garlic Butter Sauce to a serving dish.
Garnish with chopped fresh parsley.
Serve immediately, and enjoy the bright and zesty flavors of this delightful macaroni dish!

Pulled Pork Mac and Cheese

Ingredients:

- 8 ounces elbow macaroni
- 2 cups pulled pork (homemade or store-bought)
- 2 tablespoons unsalted butter
- 2 tablespoons all-purpose flour
- 2 cups milk
- 2 cups shredded sharp cheddar cheese
- 1 cup shredded mozzarella cheese
- Salt and black pepper, to taste
- 1/2 teaspoon smoked paprika
- 1/4 teaspoon cayenne pepper (optional)
- Chopped green onions (for garnish)

Instructions:

Cook the elbow macaroni according to the package instructions. Drain and set aside.
In a large saucepan, melt butter over medium heat.
Sprinkle flour over the melted butter and whisk to create a roux. Cook for 1-2 minutes.
Gradually whisk in the milk, ensuring there are no lumps. Cook and stir until the mixture thickens, about 5-7 minutes.
Add shredded sharp cheddar cheese and shredded mozzarella cheese to the sauce. Stir until the cheeses are melted and the sauce is smooth.
Season the sauce with salt, black pepper, smoked paprika, and cayenne pepper (if using).
Add the pulled pork to the sauce, stirring to combine.
Add the cooked macaroni to the cheese and pulled pork mixture, tossing to coat.
Transfer the Pulled Pork Mac and Cheese to a serving dish.
Garnish with chopped green onions.
Serve hot, and relish the comforting combination of tender pulled pork and cheesy macaroni!

Avocado and Bacon Macaroni Salad

Ingredients:

- 8 ounces elbow macaroni
- 1 avocado, diced
- 6 slices bacon, cooked and crumbled
- 1 cup cherry tomatoes, halved
- 1/2 cup red onion, finely chopped
- 1/4 cup fresh cilantro, chopped
- 1/4 cup mayonnaise
- 1/4 cup Greek yogurt
- 2 tablespoons lime juice
- Salt and black pepper, to taste
- Optional: crumbled feta cheese (for garnish)

Instructions:

Cook the elbow macaroni according to the package instructions. Drain and let it cool.

In a large bowl, combine the cooked macaroni, diced avocado, crumbled bacon, cherry tomatoes, red onion, and chopped cilantro.

In a small bowl, whisk together mayonnaise, Greek yogurt, lime juice, salt, and black pepper.

Pour the dressing over the macaroni mixture and toss to coat everything evenly.

If desired, garnish with crumbled feta cheese.

Refrigerate for at least 30 minutes before serving to allow the flavors to meld.

Serve the Avocado and Bacon Macaroni Salad chilled, and enjoy the creamy avocado, smoky bacon, and vibrant flavors!

Baked Ziti Macaroni Casserole

Ingredients:

- 1 pound ziti or penne pasta
- 1 tablespoon olive oil
- 1 onion, finely chopped
- 2 cloves garlic, minced
- 1 pound ground beef or Italian sausage
- 1 can (28 ounces) crushed tomatoes
- 1 can (14 ounces) tomato sauce
- 1 teaspoon dried oregano
- 1 teaspoon dried basil
- Salt and black pepper, to taste
- 1 cup ricotta cheese
- 1 cup shredded mozzarella cheese
- 1/2 cup grated Parmesan cheese
- Fresh basil, chopped (for garnish)

Instructions:

Preheat the oven to 375°F (190°C).
Cook the ziti or penne pasta according to the package instructions. Drain and set aside.
In a large skillet, heat olive oil over medium heat.
Add chopped onion and minced garlic to the skillet. Cook until the onion is softened.
Add ground beef or Italian sausage to the skillet and cook until browned. Drain excess fat if needed.
Stir in crushed tomatoes, tomato sauce, dried oregano, dried basil, salt, and black pepper. Simmer for about 10 minutes to allow the flavors to meld.
In a large bowl, combine the cooked pasta with the meat and tomato sauce mixture.
In a separate bowl, mix ricotta cheese, shredded mozzarella cheese, and grated Parmesan cheese.
Spread half of the pasta mixture in a greased baking dish. Dollop half of the cheese mixture over the pasta.
Add the remaining pasta mixture and top with the remaining cheese mixture.

Bake in the preheated oven for 25-30 minutes or until the cheese is melted and bubbly.

Remove from the oven and let it cool for a few minutes.

Garnish with chopped fresh basil.

Serve the Baked Ziti Macaroni Casserole warm, and enjoy the comforting layers of pasta, rich tomato sauce, and gooey cheese!

Chicken Florentine Mac and Cheese

Ingredients:

- 8 ounces elbow macaroni
- 2 boneless, skinless chicken breasts, cooked and shredded
- 2 tablespoons unsalted butter
- 2 tablespoons all-purpose flour
- 2 cups milk
- 2 cups shredded mozzarella cheese
- 1 cup grated Parmesan cheese
- 2 cups fresh spinach, chopped
- 2 cloves garlic, minced
- Salt and black pepper, to taste
- 1/4 teaspoon nutmeg
- 1/2 cup breadcrumbs
- Fresh parsley, chopped (for garnish)

Instructions:

Cook the elbow macaroni according to the package instructions. Drain and set aside.
In a large skillet, melt butter over medium heat.
Sprinkle flour over the melted butter and whisk to create a roux. Cook for 1-2 minutes.
Gradually whisk in the milk, ensuring there are no lumps. Cook and stir until the mixture thickens, about 5-7 minutes.
Add shredded mozzarella cheese and grated Parmesan cheese to the sauce. Stir until the cheeses are melted and the sauce is smooth.
In a separate pan, sauté minced garlic in a bit of olive oil until fragrant.
Add chopped fresh spinach to the garlic and cook until wilted.
Stir the cooked and shredded chicken into the cheese sauce.
Add the cooked macaroni to the sauce, tossing to coat.
Season with salt, black pepper, and nutmeg to taste.
Transfer the Chicken Florentine Mac and Cheese to a greased baking dish.
In a small bowl, mix breadcrumbs with a bit of melted butter and sprinkle over the macaroni.

Bake in a preheated oven at 375°F (190°C) for 20-25 minutes or until bubbly and golden brown on top.

Remove from the oven, sprinkle with chopped fresh parsley, and let it cool for a few minutes.

Serve this indulgent Chicken Florentine Mac and Cheese warm, and enjoy the blend of creamy cheese sauce, tender chicken, and vibrant spinach!

Macaroni with Smoky Chipotle Cheese Sauce

Ingredients:

- 8 ounces elbow macaroni
- 2 tablespoons unsalted butter
- 2 tablespoons all-purpose flour
- 2 cups milk
- 2 cups shredded sharp cheddar cheese
- 1 cup shredded smoked gouda cheese
- 1-2 chipotle peppers in adobo sauce, finely chopped (adjust to taste)
- 1 teaspoon adobo sauce (from the chipotle pepper can)
- Salt and black pepper, to taste
- 1/2 cup panko breadcrumbs
- Fresh cilantro, chopped (for garnish)

Instructions:

Cook the elbow macaroni according to the package instructions. Drain and set aside.
In a large saucepan, melt butter over medium heat.
Sprinkle flour over the melted butter and whisk to create a roux. Cook for 1-2 minutes.
Gradually whisk in the milk, ensuring there are no lumps. Cook and stir until the mixture thickens, about 5-7 minutes.
Add shredded sharp cheddar cheese and shredded smoked gouda cheese to the sauce. Stir until the cheeses are melted and the sauce is smooth.
Stir in finely chopped chipotle peppers and adobo sauce. Season with salt and black pepper to taste.
Add the cooked macaroni to the smoky chipotle cheese sauce, tossing to coat.
In a small bowl, mix panko breadcrumbs with a bit of melted butter.
Transfer the macaroni and cheese to a serving dish and sprinkle the breadcrumb mixture on top.
Garnish with chopped fresh cilantro.
Serve the Macaroni with Smoky Chipotle Cheese Sauce hot, and savor the rich and spicy combination of cheeses with a smoky kick!

Shrimp Scampi Macaroni

Ingredients:

- 8 ounces elbow macaroni
- 1 pound large shrimp, peeled and deveined
- 4 tablespoons unsalted butter
- 4 cloves garlic, minced
- 1/2 teaspoon red pepper flakes (adjust to taste)
- 1/2 cup chicken broth
- 1/4 cup dry white wine
- Juice of 1 lemon
- Salt and black pepper, to taste
- 1/4 cup fresh parsley, chopped
- 1/2 cup grated Parmesan cheese
- Lemon wedges (for serving)

Instructions:

Cook the elbow macaroni according to the package instructions. Drain and set aside.
Season the shrimp with salt and black pepper.
In a large skillet, melt 2 tablespoons of butter over medium-high heat.
Add the shrimp to the skillet and cook until pink, about 2-3 minutes per side.
Remove the shrimp from the skillet and set aside.
In the same skillet, add the remaining 2 tablespoons of butter.
Sauté minced garlic and red pepper flakes until the garlic is fragrant.
Pour in chicken broth, white wine, and lemon juice. Bring the mixture to a simmer.
Add the cooked macaroni to the skillet and toss to coat in the sauce.
Stir in the cooked shrimp and chopped fresh parsley.
Sprinkle grated Parmesan cheese over the top and stir until the cheese is melted and the sauce is creamy.
Season with additional salt and black pepper if needed.
Serve the Shrimp Scampi Macaroni hot, garnished with extra parsley and lemon wedges for squeezing over the dish. Enjoy the delightful combination of tender shrimp and zesty scampi flavors with macaroni!

Tomato Basil Pesto Mac and Cheese

Ingredients:

- 8 ounces elbow macaroni
- 2 tablespoons unsalted butter
- 2 tablespoons all-purpose flour
- 2 cups milk
- 2 cups shredded sharp cheddar cheese
- 1/2 cup grated Parmesan cheese
- 1/4 cup tomato paste
- 1/4 cup basil pesto
- Salt and black pepper, to taste
- 1/2 cup cherry tomatoes, halved
- Fresh basil, chopped (for garnish)

Instructions:

Cook the elbow macaroni according to the package instructions. Drain and set aside.
In a large saucepan, melt butter over medium heat.
Sprinkle flour over the melted butter and whisk to create a roux. Cook for 1-2 minutes.
Gradually whisk in the milk, ensuring there are no lumps. Cook and stir until the mixture thickens, about 5-7 minutes.
Add shredded sharp cheddar cheese and grated Parmesan cheese to the sauce. Stir until the cheeses are melted and the sauce is smooth.
Stir in tomato paste and basil pesto until well combined.
Season with salt and black pepper to taste.
Add the cooked macaroni to the tomato basil pesto cheese sauce, tossing to coat.
Gently fold in halved cherry tomatoes.
Serve the Tomato Basil Pesto Mac and Cheese hot, garnished with chopped fresh basil. Enjoy the vibrant flavors of tomato, basil, and cheesy goodness in every bite!

Macaroni with White Wine and Mushroom Sauce

Ingredients:

- 8 ounces elbow macaroni
- 2 tablespoons olive oil
- 1 pound cremini mushrooms, sliced
- 4 cloves garlic, minced
- 1/2 cup dry white wine
- 1 cup heavy cream
- 1 cup grated Parmesan cheese
- Salt and black pepper, to taste
- Fresh parsley, chopped (for garnish)

Instructions:

Cook the elbow macaroni according to the package instructions. Drain and set aside.

In a large skillet, heat olive oil over medium heat.

Add sliced cremini mushrooms to the skillet and sauté until they release their moisture and become golden brown.

Stir in minced garlic and cook for an additional minute until fragrant.

Pour in dry white wine and let it simmer for 2-3 minutes to reduce.

Add heavy cream to the skillet and bring the mixture to a gentle simmer.

Stir in grated Parmesan cheese, allowing it to melt into the sauce. Season with salt and black pepper to taste.

Add the cooked macaroni to the mushroom and white wine sauce, tossing to coat.

Serve the Macaroni with White Wine and Mushroom Sauce hot, garnished with chopped fresh parsley. Enjoy the rich and savory combination of mushrooms, white wine, and creamy Parmesan sauce with macaroni!

Italian Sausage and Kale Macaroni Bake

Ingredients:

- 8 ounces elbow macaroni
- 1 pound Italian sausage, casings removed
- 1 tablespoon olive oil
- 1 onion, finely chopped
- 3 cloves garlic, minced
- 1 bunch kale, stems removed and leaves chopped
- 1 can (28 ounces) crushed tomatoes
- 1 teaspoon dried oregano
- 1 teaspoon dried basil
- Salt and black pepper, to taste
- 2 cups shredded mozzarella cheese
- 1/2 cup grated Parmesan cheese
- Fresh basil, chopped (for garnish)

Instructions:

Cook the elbow macaroni according to the package instructions. Drain and set aside.

In a large skillet, cook the Italian sausage over medium-high heat, breaking it apart with a spoon as it cooks. Once browned, remove excess fat and set aside.

In the same skillet, add olive oil and chopped onion. Sauté until the onion is translucent.

Add minced garlic to the skillet and cook for an additional minute until fragrant. Stir in chopped kale and cook until wilted.

Add crushed tomatoes, dried oregano, dried basil, salt, and black pepper to the skillet. Bring the mixture to a simmer and cook for 10-15 minutes.

Preheat your oven to 375°F (190°C).

In a large mixing bowl, combine the cooked macaroni, browned Italian sausage, and tomato-kale sauce. Mix well.

Transfer half of the macaroni mixture to a baking dish. Sprinkle half of the shredded mozzarella and Parmesan cheeses over the top.

Add the remaining macaroni mixture to the baking dish and cover with the remaining cheeses.

Bake in the preheated oven for 20-25 minutes or until the cheese is melted and bubbly.

Garnish with chopped fresh basil before serving.
Serve the Italian Sausage and Kale Macaroni Bake hot, savoring the hearty flavors of sausage, kale, and cheesy goodness!